CYBER HEORES

KIDS DEFENDING THE DIGITAL REALM

WRITTEN BY

DR. VALARIAN COUCH

Copyright © 2024 by Dr. Valarian Couch

All rights reserved. No part of this publication may be reproduced, distributed, or transmitted in any form or by any means, including photocopying, recording, or other electronic or mechanical methods, without the prior written permission of the publisher, except in the case of brief quotations embodied in critical reviews and certain other noncommercial uses permitted by copyright law.

For permission requests, write to the publisher at the address below.

[valarian.couch@gmail.com]

Acknowledgments

Writing this book has been an incredible journey, and it wouldn't have been possible without the support and encouragement of many people.

First and foremost, I want to express my deepest gratitude to my family. Your unwavering belief in my vision and constant support provided the foundation upon which this book was built. To my wife, for your patience and love, and to my children, who remind me every day of the importance of pursuing one's passions – thank you from the bottom of my heart.

A special thanks goes to my colleagues and peers in the cybersecurity and AI communities. Your insights, feedback, and spirited discussions have been invaluable.

Lastly, to you, the readers, who share a keen interest in the world of AI and cybersecurity – this book is for you. Your eagerness to learn and evolve in this ever-changing field is what drives authors like myself to share our knowledge and experiences. I hope this book provides you with valuable insights and aids in your journey in AI and cybersecurity.

Thank you all for being part of this incredible journey.

DR. VALARIAN COUCH

TABLE OF CONTENTS

INTRODUCTION TO AI IN CYBERSECURITY 6
CHAPTER 1: MEET THE CYBER HEROES 8
CHAPTER 2: THE MYSTERIOUS EMAIL 12
    Receiving the Email 12
    The Click 14
    Introduction of the Immediate Consequences 15
    Cleaning Up the Tablets 17
    Learning from the Experience 18
CHAPTER 3: ENTER DR. BYTE 20
    Introduction of Dr. Byte 20
    Explanation of Phishing 22
    First Lesson 23
CHAPTER 4: THE DIGITAL WORLD 26
    Entering the Digital World 26
    Exploration and Discovery 28
    Meeting New Friends 32
CHAPTER 5: THE PHISHER'S TRAP 35
    The First Encounter 35
    Using Their Knowledge 39
CHAPTER 6: THE HACKER'S CHALLENGE 43
    Introduction of Hackster 43
    Hackster's Plan 45
    Dealing with Hackster 47
Chapter 7: Strengthening Defenses 51

Learning Advanced Techniques 51
Practice Makes Perfect 54
CHAPTER 8: THE FINAL BATTLE 58
Phisher and Hackster Team Up 58
The Cyber Heroes' Strategy 59
The Showdown 60
CHAPTER 9: VICTORY AND CELEBRATION 66
Defeating the Villains 66
Returning Home 68
Spreading the Word 71
CHAPTER 10: EPILOGUE – BE A CYBER HERO 74
Reflecting on the Journey 74
Encouraging Others 75
Final Words from Dr. Byte 78

INTRODUCTION TO AI IN CYBERSECURITY

Artificial intelligence (AI) is transforming the world of cybersecurity, providing new tools and ways to combat the constantly changing threats online. Imagine machines that can learn, adapt, and make decisions independently to safeguard our digital information. This is what AI brings to cybersecurity.

AI analyzes huge/large amounts of data in real time, spotting unusual activities and potential security risks more quickly and accurately than older methods.

One major advantage of using AI in cybersecurity is its ability to handle repetitive tasks, allowing human analysts to focus on more complex security issues. This makes security teams more productive and effective, helping them stay ahead of threats and reduce the damage from attacks.

However, AI is not a perfect solution. There are challenges and issues to consider when incorporating AI into cybersecurity strategies. A significant concern is the possibility that AI systems could be manipulated by skilled attackers. This underscores the need for thorough testing and validation to ensure that AI-driven security systems are reliable and accurate.

Ethical and privacy concerns are also important when using AI in cybersecurity. It's essential to carefully manage issues like data privacy, transparency, and accountability to maintain trust among users and stakeholders. Balancing the benefits of AI with these ethical considerations is crucial.

In the fast-paced realm of cybersecurity, keeping up with the latest AI developments and how they can protect against cyber threats is vital. By understanding AI's potential and the associated challenges, we can leverage this technology to build a safer and more secure digital world for everyone.

CHAPTER 1: MEET THE CYBER HEROES

Max and Luna were best friends who shared a love for adventure and technology. Max, with his curly brown hair and bright blue eyes, was always curious and eager to learn new things. He loved exploring the world around him, whether it was the physical world or the vast expanse of the internet. Luna, on the other hand, had long black hair tied into a neat ponytail and sparkling green eyes. She was a problem solver, always ready to tackle any challenge that came her way. Together, they made the perfect team.

Max and Luna spent countless hours after school playing games on their tablets. They loved discovering new apps, solving puzzles, and competing in friendly challenges. Their favorite game was "Cyber Quest," a digital adventure where they could explore different worlds and complete missions. They were always on the lookout for new and exciting games to play, and their tablets were their gateways to endless fun and learning.

One sunny morning, Max and Luna arrived at school buzzing with excitement. Today was a special day – their class was starting a new project that involved using tablets to learn about different subjects. Their teacher, Mrs. Thompson, had told them that they would be working in teams to create presentations on various topics using the school's tablets. Max and Luna couldn't wait to get started.

As they walked into the classroom, they were greeted by their classmates. There was Sam, who loved drawing and was always doodling in his notebook; Emily, who was the fastest runner in their grade and loved playing sports; and Alex, who could solve any math problem in the blink of an eye. Mrs. Thompson, a kind and patient teacher with a warm smile, welcomed them all and explained the project in detail.

"Good morning, everyone!" Mrs. Thompson began. "Today, we're starting a very exciting project. We'll be using tablets to explore different subjects and create presentations. You'll work in teams, and each team will choose a topic to research. Then, you'll use the tablets to gather information, create slides, and present your findings to the class."

Max and Luna exchanged thrilled glances. They loved working on projects together, and the idea of using tablets made it even more exciting. They quickly formed a team and began brainstorming ideas for their project.

"We should do something related to technology," Max suggested. "Maybe we can explore how different gadgets work or the history of computers."

Luna nodded enthusiastically. "That sounds great! We could also look into internet safety and how to stay safe online. It's something we both care about, and it could be really helpful for everyone."

With their topic decided, Max and Luna eagerly started their research. They opened their tablets and began exploring different websites and videos that explained the basics of internet safety. They learned about creating strong passwords, recognizing safe websites, and avoiding suspicious links. As they gathered information, they made notes and started planning their presentation.

The classroom buzzed with activity as all the teams worked on their projects. Sam was sketching diagrams for his team's presentation on the solar system, Emily was researching famous athletes for her team's sports project, and Alex was calculating data for his team's math-related presentation. Mrs. Thompson walked around the room, offering guidance and answering questions.

Max and Luna were so engrossed in their research that they didn't notice the time passing. Before they knew it, the school day was almost over. Mrs. Thompson called the class to attention and asked everyone to share a brief update on their projects.

"Max and Luna, would you like to go first?" she asked.

Max and Luna stood up and shared their idea with the class. "We're working on a project about internet safety," Max began. "We've been learning about how to create strong passwords, recognize safe websites, and avoid phishing scams."

Luna added, "We think it's really important for everyone to know how to stay safe online, especially since we all use tablets and computers so much. We're excited to share what we've learned with all of you."

Their classmates listened intently, and Mrs. Thompson gave them an encouraging smile. "That's a fantastic topic, Max and Luna. I'm sure your presentation will be very informative and helpful for everyone."

As the school day ended, Max and Luna felt a sense of accomplishment. They were excited about the progress they had made and eager to continue their project. Little did they know that their journey into the world of cybersecurity was just beginning, and they would soon become real-life Cyber Heroes.

CHAPTER 2: THE MYSTERIOUS EMAIL

Receiving the Email

Max and Luna were best friends. They loved playing games on their tablets. One sunny afternoon, after finishing their homework, they decided to play a game, **"Castle Adventures."**

Max was excitedly battling dragons and building castles when a notification popped up on his screen. "You've got mail!" it said.

Max clicked on the email and saw a message that made his eyes sparkle with excitement.

"FREE GAME POINTS! Click here to get 1,000 points for Castle Adventures!" the email read. The message was colorful, with pictures of treasure chests and shiny game points.

"Hey, Luna, come and see this!" Max called out.

Luna walked over and looked at the email on Max's tablet. She frowned. "I don't know, Max. This looks a bit strange. Why would someone give away game points for free?"

Max shrugged. "Maybe it's a special offer. It looks so cool! Imagine all the things we could buy in the game!"

Luna was still skeptical but curious. "I guess it wouldn't hurt to take a look. But let's be careful, okay?"

Max nodded. "Okay, let's check it out together."

The Click

Max and Luna sat side by side and clicked the link in the email. As soon as they did, their screens started to flicker. The once smooth and colorful graphics of "Castle Adventures" began to glitch.

"Uh-oh," Max said, his voice trembling a little. "This doesn't look right."

Suddenly, pop-ups started appearing all over their screens. "Congratulations! You've won a prize!" one pop-up announced. Another one flashed, "Click here to claim your reward!"

Max and Luna exchanged worried glances. The game became slower and slower, and their tablets made strange buzzing noises.

"This is really bad," Luna said. "I think we might have done something wrong."

Just then, their screens went completely black. For a moment, everything was silent. Then, a new figure appeared on their screens. It was a cartoon character with a big, friendly smile and glasses that looked like computer screens.

"Hello, kids!" the character said. "My name is Dr. Byte, and it looks like you might need some help."

Introduction of the Immediate Consequences

Max and Luna were both a little scared but also curious. "Who are you?" Max asked.

"I'm Dr. Byte, a Cyber Hero," the character said. "I help kids learn how to stay safe online. It looks like you clicked on a phishing link."

"A phishing links?" Luna asked. "What's that?"

Dr. Byte nodded. "Phishing is when someone tries to trick you into giving away your personal information or clicking on a link that can harm your device. It's like when a fisherman uses bait to catch fish. But instead of fish, these bad guys are trying to catch your information."

Max's eyes widened. "So that's why our tablets are acting weird?"

"Exactly," Dr. Byte said. "When you clicked on that link, it started to put bad stuff, called malware, onto your tablets. That's why you're seeing all those pop-ups and why your game isn't working right."

Luna frowned. "What can we do to fix it?"

"Don't worry," Dr. Byte reassured them. "I'll guide you through the steps to clean up your tablets and show you how to avoid these kinds of tricks in the future. But first, let's take a closer look at what happened."

Dr. Byte waved his hand, and the screens of Max and Luna's tablets showed a series of images explaining the consequences of clicking on suspicious links.

"See these pop-ups?" Dr. Byte pointed at the flashing ads. "They are trying to get you to click on more links so they can cause more trouble. It's important not to click on them."

Max and Luna nodded, paying close attention.

"Your tablets are also running slowly because the malware is using up your tablet's power to do bad things," Dr. Byte continued. "And if you had entered any personal information, like your name or address, the bad guys would have taken it."

Max felt a bit scared. "That's really bad. I didn't know something like this could happen."

"It's okay, Max," Dr. Byte said kindly. "That's why I'm here to help. We all make mistakes, and the important thing is to learn from them."

Luna looked at Dr. Byte. "So, what do we do now?"

Dr. Byte smiled. "First, we need to clean up your tablets. Then, I'll teach you some simple ways to stay safe online. Are you ready to become Cyber Heroes?"

Max and Luna nodded eagerly. They were ready to learn and fix their mistake.

Cleaning Up the Tablets

Dr. Byte guided Max and Luna through the steps to clean up their tablets. They followed along carefully.

"First, we need to close all those pop-ups," Dr. Byte instructed. "But be careful not to click on anything inside them. Just close them using the little 'X' at the top."

Max and Luna carefully closed all the pop-ups. It took a while, but eventually, their screens were clear.

"Great job!" Dr. Byte cheered. "Now, let's check for any apps that might have been installed without your permission. Go to your settings and look at the list of apps."

Max and Luna opened their settings and scanned through their apps. They found a few they didn't recognize.

"These must be the bad apps," Max said.

"Exactly," Dr. Byte confirmed. "Delete them right away."

They deleted the suspicious apps, feeling more confident with each step.

"Now, let's make sure there are no strange extensions on your browsers," Dr. Byte continued. "Go to your browser settings and check the extensions."

Max and Luna found and removed a couple of strange extensions.

"Almost done!" Dr. Byte said. "The last step is to run a security scan. Do you have a security app installed?"

Max and Luna both nodded. They opened their security apps and ran full scans. The apps found and removed the remaining malware.

"All clean!" Dr. Byte announced. "You've done a fantastic job."

Max and Luna high-fived each other. Their tablets were back to normal, and they felt relieved.

Learning from the Experience

"Now that your tablets are safe, let's talk about how to avoid this happening again," Dr. Byte said. "There are a few simple rules to follow."

Max and Luna listened carefully.

"First, always be suspicious of emails or messages that offer something too good to be true, like free game points," Dr. Byte explained. "If it seems too good to be true, it probably is."

Luna nodded. "We should have known. It did seem a bit strange."

"Exactly," Dr. Byte said. "Second, never click on links or download attachments from people you don't know. If you're not sure, ask an adult for help."

Max agreed. "We'll definitely do that from now on."

"And third," Dr. Byte continued, "use strong passwords and change them regularly. Also, make sure your security software is always up to date."

Max and Luna felt empowered with their new knowledge.

"Thank you, Dr. Byte," Luna said. "We learned so much today."

"You're welcome," Dr. Byte said. "Remember, you are now Cyber Heroes. It's your job to stay safe online and help others do the same."

Max and Luna smiled proudly. They couldn't wait to share what they had learned with their friends and family.

"Now, go and enjoy your game, but stay safe!" Dr. Byte said with a wink.

Max and Luna waved goodbye to Dr. Byte and returned to "Castle Adventures," ready to play and help their friends become Cyber Heroes too.

CHAPTER 3: ENTER DR. BYTE

Introduction of Dr. Byte

Max and Luna stared at their screens, still in shock from the strange email and the chaos it caused. The friendly cartoon character with glasses that looked like computer screens smiled warmly at them.

"Hello, kids!" the character said. "My name is Dr. Byte, and I'm here to help you."

Max and Luna exchanged puzzled looks. "Who are you?" Max asked.

"I'm Dr. Byte, a Cyber Hero," the character replied. "I help kids like you learn how to stay safe online."

Luna tilted her head, curiosity evident in her eyes. "A Cyber Hero? What do you do exactly?"

Dr. Byte's smile grew wider. "I teach important lessons about the internet and how to avoid dangers like phishing and hacking. It's like being a superhero, but in the digital world!"

Max's eyes sparkled with excitement. "Wow, that's so cool! Can you help us fix our tablets?"

"Absolutely," Dr. Byte said. "But first, let's talk about what happened and why it happened."

Explanation of Phishing

Dr. Byte pulled up a large screen that appeared to hover in front of Max and Luna's tablets. On the screen, there were colorful pictures and simple words to explain things clearly.

"Phishing," Dr. Byte began, "is when someone tries to trick you into giving away your personal information or clicking on a link that can harm your device. It's like a fisherman using bait to catch fish, but instead of fish, these bad guys are trying to catch your information."

The screen showed a cartoon fisherman casting a line with a bait labeled "Free Game Points." The bait was snapped up by a fish labeled "Max."

Max blushed a little. "So, that email we clicked on was bait?"

"Exactly," Dr. Byte confirmed. "The email promised you free game points to make you click on the link. Once you did, the bad guys could put harmful software, called malware, on your tablet."

Luna frowned. "But how do they know what to send us?"

Dr. Byte nodded. "Good question, Luna. These bad guys often guess what kids like you might be interested in, like games or cool new apps. They make their emails look very tempting, but there are usually signs that something isn't right."

The screen changed to show a list of signs:

- The email address looks strange.
- The message offers something too good to be true.

- There are spelling or grammar mistakes.
- The link doesn't match the website's real address.

"These are some clues that an email might be a phishing attempt," Dr. Byte explained. "Always look for these signs before clicking on any links."

First Lesson

Max and Luna leaned forward, eager to learn more.

"Now," Dr. Byte said, "let's learn our first lesson on how to protect ourselves from phishing."

The screen showed a bright, animated classroom with Dr. Byte at the front, and Max and Luna sitting at desks.

"Lesson one," Dr. Byte began, "is to never click on links or download attachments from people you don't know. Even if it looks exciting, it's better to be safe and ask an adult if you're unsure."

Max raised his hand, just like he would in a real classroom. "What if the email looks really real, like it's from our favorite game?"

"Great question, Max," Dr. Byte said. "Sometimes, phishing emails can look very real. That's why it's important to check the email address carefully and look for those clues we talked about. If you're ever unsure, visit the official website directly instead of clicking the link."

Luna tapped her chin thoughtfully. "What if it's from someone we know, but it still looks weird?"

Dr. Byte nodded. "Phishers can sometimes make it look like the email is from someone you know. If an email from a friend looks strange or asks for personal information, contact your friend directly to check if it's real."

The screen then displayed a big, colorful shield with a lock in the middle. "Lesson two," Dr. Byte continued, "is to use strong passwords and change them regularly. A strong password is like a strong shield that protects your information."

"How do we make a strong password?" Max asked.

"Use a mix of letters, numbers, and symbols," Dr. Byte explained. "Make it something you can remember but hard for others to guess. For example, instead of using 'password123', use something like 'P@ssw0rd!23'."

Max and Luna practiced creating strong passwords with Dr. Byte's guidance. They giggled as they came up with creative and secure passwords.

"Lesson three," Dr. Byte said, "is to always keep your security software up to date. Just like a superhero needs to stay in top shape, your tablet needs to have the latest updates to fight off new threats."

The screen showed a superhero tablet with a cape, flexing its muscles. Max and Luna laughed at the image.

"Finally," Dr. Byte said, "remember to always be cautious and think before you click. If something feels off, trust your instincts and ask for help."

Max and Luna felt a wave of confidence wash over them. They had learned so much in such a short time, and they were ready to be Cyber Heroes.

"Thank you, Dr. Byte," Luna said. "We learned a lot today."

"You're very welcome," Dr. Byte replied. "Remember, I'm always here to help you. You can call on me anytime you need advice or have questions about staying safe online."

Max and Luna smiled. They felt a connection with Dr. Byte and knew they could rely on him for guidance. They were eager to share what they had learned with their friends and family.

"Now," Dr. Byte said with a wink, "let's go back and play your game safely. And remember, you are now Cyber Heroes. It's your job to stay safe and help others do the same."

Max and Luna waved goodbye to Dr. Byte as he disappeared from their screens. They felt proud and ready to take on any online challenges that came their way.

CHAPTER 4: THE DIGITAL WORLD

Entering the Digital World

Max and Luna were eager to learn more from Dr. Byte. They had just learned about phishing and how to protect themselves, but they knew there was more to discover.

Dr. Byte appeared on their screens again, smiling warmly. "Hello again, Max and Luna. Are you ready for your next adventure?"

Max and Luna nodded enthusiastically. "Yes, we are!"

Cyber Heroes

"Great!" Dr. Byte said. "This time, we're going to explore the digital world. There, you'll learn about different cyber threats and how to stay safe from them."

With a wave of his hand, Dr. Byte's image grew larger and brighter until it filled the entire screen. The colors on their screens swirled and danced around them. Max and Luna felt a strange sensation, like they were being pulled into their tablets. Their bodies tingled as if they were floating in a bubble. Before they knew it, they were standing in a colorful, digital landscape.

The digital world was unlike anything they had ever seen. The sky was a brilliant shade of blue, with clouds made of floating data bits. Tall, shimmering buildings with neon lights surrounded them. Streams of data flowed like rivers, winding through the landscape and disappearing into the horizon.

"Wow," Max said, his eyes wide with wonder. "This place is amazing!"

"It sure is," Luna agreed, spinning around to take in the view. "Look at all the colors!"

Dr. Byte chuckled, floating beside them. "Welcome to the digital world, kids! Here, you'll learn about different cyber threats and how to protect yourselves from them."

Max and Luna took a few steps forward, their feet feeling light as they walked on the glowing, pixelated ground. They could see various icons floating around them, each representing different parts of the internet.

"Follow me," Dr. Byte said, leading the way. "Our first stop is the Email Building."

Exploration and Discovery

Max and Luna looked around in awe. The digital world was bright and vibrant, filled with floating icons and streams of data flowing like rivers. They could see towering skyscrapers made of glowing circuits and paths paved with binary code. The air buzzed with the sounds of whirring processors and beeping notifications.

"Wow," Max said, his eyes wide with wonder. "This place is amazing!"

"It sure is," Luna agreed. "But what are we supposed to do here?"

Dr. Byte appeared beside them, looking just as cheerful as ever. "Welcome to the digital world, kids! Here, you'll learn about different cyber threats and how to protect yourselves from them."

Max and Luna followed Dr. Byte as he led them through the digital landscape. They passed by various buildings labeled with words like "Emails," "Websites," and "Games."

"Our first stop is the Email Building," Dr. Byte said. "Inside, you'll learn more about phishing and other email threats."

Inside the Email Building, Max and Luna saw screens displaying different types of emails. Dr. Byte pointed to a screen showing a suspicious email.

"Remember this?" he asked. "This is the kind of email you should watch out for. But there are other email threats too, like spam and attachments that can carry malware."

The screens changed to show examples of spam emails and harmful attachments. Max and Luna watched carefully, taking mental notes.

"Spam emails are like junk mail," Dr. Byte explained. "They fill up your inbox with unwanted messages. And some attachments can have malware, which can harm your device."

Max raised his hand. "So, we should delete spam emails and not open strange attachments?"

"Exactly," Dr. Byte confirmed. "And always be careful with links. If you don't know the sender, don't click on them."

Next, they walked to a nearby building labeled "Websites." Inside, they saw screens showing different websites. Some looked professional and secure, while others looked suspicious and untrustworthy.

"Not all websites are safe," Dr. Byte explained. "Some can steal your information or install malware on your device. Always make sure the website's address starts with 'https://' and has a padlock icon next to it. This means the site is secure."

Max and Luna nodded, committing this important information to memory. The screen showed a website with a padlock icon and another without it.

Dr. Byte pointed to the screen. "The padlock means the site uses encryption to protect your information. Always look for it before entering personal details."

"Got it," Luna said. "We'll be careful about which sites we visit."

"Now, let's move on to the Game Building," Dr. Byte said. Max and Luna followed him eagerly, excited to learn more.

Inside the Game Building, Max and Luna saw screens displaying various games. Some screens showed games with bright, flashy ads promising rewards.

"Be careful with ads in games," Dr. Byte warned. "Some can lead to harmful websites or ask for personal information. Always check with an adult before clicking on any ads."

Max nodded thoughtfully. "I used to click on those ads all the time. Now I know better."

Luna agreed. "We'll be more careful from now on."

Dr. Byte continued to guide them through different parts of the digital world. They visited the Social Media Building, where they learned about the dangers of sharing too much information online.

"Only share information with people you trust," Dr. Byte advised. "And always check your privacy settings to make sure your profile is secure."

The screen showed a cartoon character sharing too much information and the consequences of it. Max and Luna understood the importance of keeping their personal information private.

Next, they went to the App Building. Inside, they discovered how to download apps safely and avoid malicious ones. Cyber Pet sniffed out a suspicious app and barked, warning them to stay away.

"Always download apps from trusted sources," Dr. Byte said. "And read the reviews to see if other users had problems."

Max and Luna were starting to feel more confident. They were learning a lot and felt ready to face any cyber threat. They continued their exploration, visiting various buildings and learning valuable lessons about cyber safety.

Meeting New Friends

As they continued their journey through the digital world, Dr. Byte introduced Max and Luna to some new friends who would help them on their quest.

First, they met Cyber Pet, a cute, robot-like dog with shiny fur and bright, glowing eyes. Cyber Pet wagged its tail happily and barked a friendly greeting.

"This is Cyber Pet," Dr. Byte said. "He will help you by sniffing out any suspicious activity. If Cyber Pet barks, it means there's something you need to check."

Max bent down to pet Cyber Pet, who responded with happy barks. "Nice to meet you, Cyber Pet!" Max said.

Next, they met Cyber Guide, a friendly character who looked like a wise old owl with glasses. Cyber Guide flapped his wings and perched on a nearby branch.

"Hello, children," Cyber Guide said in a warm, gentle voice. "I'm here to provide you with information and tips whenever you need them. Just ask me anything about staying safe online."

Luna smiled at Cyber Guide. "Thank you! We'll definitely need your help."

Together with their new friends, Max and Luna continued to explore the digital world. They visited more buildings, each one teaching them about different cyber threats.

In the Social Media Building, they learned about the dangers of sharing too much information online. Cyber Guide explained how to set their privacy settings to keep their profiles safe.

In the App Building, they discovered how to download apps safely and avoid malicious ones. Cyber Pet sniffed out a suspicious app and barked, warning them to stay away.

Every step of the way, Dr. Byte, Cyber Pet, and Cyber Guide were there to help and guide them. Max and Luna felt more confident and knowledgeable with each lesson.

After a long day of exploring and learning, Dr. Byte gathered Max and Luna for a final lesson.

"Today, you've learned a lot about staying safe online," Dr. Byte said. "Remember to always be cautious, think before you click, and use the tools and tips we've talked about. With these skills, you can be true Cyber Heroes."

Max and Luna smiled proudly. They felt ready to take on any challenge the digital world might throw at them.

"Thank you, Dr. Byte," Max said. "And thank you, Cyber Pet and Cyber Guide. You've taught us so much."

"You're very welcome," Dr. Byte replied. "Remember, we're always here to help you. Just call on us whenever you need advice or support."

Max and Luna waved goodbye to their new friends as they felt the familiar sensation of being pulled back to the real world. In an instant, they were back in their room, holding their tablets.

But now, they were different. They were Cyber Heroes, ready to protect themselves and others from the dangers of the digital world.

CHAPTER 5: THE PHISHER'S TRAP

The First Encounter

Max and Luna were eager to be back in the digital world. They had learned so much from Dr. Byte and felt ready to face any challenge. The digital landscape was even more vibrant and exciting than before, with new buildings and paths they hadn't explored yet.

As they walked, Cyber Pet trotted happily beside them, occasionally sniffing the air as if sensing something. Cyber Guide flew overhead, keeping a watchful eye on their surroundings.

"Look at all these new places to explore," Max said, pointing to a series of colorful buildings labeled "Games," "Apps," and "Social Media."

"Yeah, it's like a whole new adventure waiting for us," Luna replied, her eyes sparkling with excitement.

Just then, Cyber Pet began barking and sniffing around a nearby alleyway. Max and Luna followed, curious to see what had caught Cyber Pet's attention.

In the shadows of the alley, they saw a figure with a fishing rod, casting lines into the data streams that flowed like rivers through the digital world. The figure was dressed in dark, tattered clothes, and his eyes gleamed with mischief.

"Who is that?" Max asked, his eyes narrowing as he tried to get a better look.

Dr. Byte frowned, stepping closer to Max and Luna. "That's Phisher, one of the digital world's biggest troublemakers. He tries to trick people into giving away their information."

Luna's eyes widened with recognition. "Phisher? Like the phishing emails we learned about?"

"Exactly," Dr. Byte said. "He's very crafty, so you need to stay alert and use everything you've learned."

Phisher noticed them and smirked. He pulled out a shiny bait that looked very tempting. It was a pop-up offering free game points and cool upgrades, just like the email Max had received before.

"Hey, kids!" Phisher called out, waving the bait enticingly. "Want some free game points? Just click this link!"

Max and Luna exchanged worried glances. They remembered Dr. Byte's lessons and knew they had to be careful. The bait looked tempting, but they had learned the importance of thinking before clicking.

"Those points look so tempting," Max said, staring at the bait. "But we know better now."

Phisher's smirk grew wider. "Come on, just a little click. It won't hurt, I promise."

Luna stepped forward, shaking her head. "No, Phisher. We know your tricks. We're not falling for it."

Phisher's eyes narrowed, and he pulled out another bait, this time a colorful ad for a new game. "How about this, then? A brand-new game, absolutely free! Just one click away."

Max and Luna looked at the ad, and for a moment, they were tempted. But they remembered what Dr. Byte had taught them about suspicious links.

Max took a deep breath and steadied himself. "Let's check the link first. Remember what Dr. Byte said."

Luna nodded, agreeing. "Yes, let's be careful."

They inspected the link carefully. Sure enough, it didn't have the padlock or the 'https://' at the beginning. Max shook his head firmly.

"No, Phisher. We're not clicking that link either."

Phisher's face turned red with frustration. "You think you're so smart, don't you? Well, let's see if you can handle this!"

With a flick of his wrist, Phisher cast multiple lines at once, filling the air with pop-ups and ads. The digital world around them seemed to buzz with confusion, as if the very data streams were agitated by the malicious activity.

Max and Luna stayed calm. They remembered Dr. Byte's lessons about staying cautious and thinking before clicking. They ignored the pop-ups and focused on finding the source of the problem.

"Cyber Pet, can you help us?" Luna called out, her voice steady despite the chaos.

Cyber Pet barked and sniffed around, quickly identifying the lines that were causing the most trouble. Max and Luna followed Cyber Pet's lead, tracing the lines back to their source.

"There!" Max pointed; his eyes sharp. "That's where Phisher's hiding his traps."

Dr. Byte nodded; his expression serious. "Great job, kids. Now, use what you've learned to deactivate the traps."

Max and Luna carefully approached the source of the lines. They used their knowledge to close the pop-ups and block the suspicious links. They double-checked each step, making sure they didn't accidentally click on anything harmful.

Finally, they managed to deactivate the last trap. The digital world around them calmed down, and the pop-ups disappeared. Phisher looked furious.

"You may have won this time, but I'll be back!" he shouted before vanishing into the shadows, leaving behind a quiet, peaceful digital landscape.

Using Their Knowledge

Max and Luna took a deep breath, feeling a mix of relief and pride. They had successfully avoided Phisher's traps and protected themselves from the phishing scam.

Dr. Byte smiled proudly. "Well done, Cyber Heroes! You used your knowledge and stayed calm under pressure. That's exactly what you should do in situations like this."

Cyber Pet wagged his tail, barking happily. Cyber Guide nodded approvingly. "You handled that very well. Remember, staying cautious and thinking before you click are the keys to staying safe online."

Max grinned, feeling a sense of accomplishment. "We did it, Luna! We outsmarted Phisher!"

Luna smiled back, her confidence growing. "Yeah, and we learned so much. This was our first real test, and we passed."

Dr. Byte gathered them together for a quick review. "Let's go over what you did right. First, you identified the signs of a phishing scam. You recognized that the offers were too good to be true and checked the links carefully."

Max and Luna listened intently, soaking in the praise and the valuable lessons.

"Second," Dr. Byte continued, "you stayed calm and didn't panic when Phisher tried to overwhelm you with pop-ups. You ignored the distractions and focused on finding the source of the problem."

Max nodded. "We remembered what you taught us about not clicking on anything suspicious."

Luna added, "And we used Cyber Pet to help us find the traps. That made it easier to trace them back to Phisher."

"Exactly," Dr. Byte said with a smile. "You worked together as a team, used your resources, and applied your knowledge. Those are the qualities of true Cyber Heroes."

Max and Luna felt a warm glow of pride. They knew they had made the right choices and were becoming true Cyber Heroes. The confidence they felt now would help them face any future challenges in the digital world.

As they walked back through the digital world, Max and Luna reflected on their adventure. They had faced a real cyber threat and emerged victorious. They felt more confident and ready to tackle any future challenges.

"Thank you, Dr. Byte," Max said. "We couldn't have done it without your guidance."

Dr. Byte smiled. "You're very welcome, Max. But remember, the real power lies within you. You've learned a lot, and now you have the skills to stay safe online."

Luna nodded, feeling a sense of responsibility. "And we'll share what we learned with our friends and family. We want everyone to be safe online."

Dr. Byte's smile widened. "That's the spirit of a true Cyber Hero. Keep spreading the knowledge and helping others."

Max and Luna waved goodbye to Dr. Byte, Cyber Pet, and Cyber Guide as they felt the familiar sensation of being pulled back to the real world. In an instant, they were back in their room, holding their tablets.

But now, they were different. They were Cyber Heroes, ready to protect themselves and others from the dangers of the digital world.

They looked at each other and smiled. "We did it," Max said. "We really did it."

Luna nodded. "And this is just the beginning. There's so much more to learn and share."

Max agreed. "Let's make sure we always stay vigilant and help others do the same."

With that, Max and Luna returned to their game, feeling more confident and knowledgeable. They were no longer just players; they were Cyber Heroes, ready to face any challenge and keep the digital world safe.

CHAPTER 6: THE HACKER'S CHALLENGE

Introduction of Hackster

Max and Luna were enjoying their newfound confidence as Cyber Heroes. They had learned so much from Dr. Byte and had successfully dealt with Phisher. But their adventures in the digital world were far from over.

One day, as they explored a new area of the digital world filled with colorful data streams and floating icons, Cyber Pet suddenly started barking. Cyber Guide flew down and landed beside them, looking worried.

"What's wrong, Cyber Pet?" Max asked, kneeling to pat the robotic dog's head.

Cyber Guide's eyes narrowed behind his glasses. "It looks like we're about to face a new challenge. A very tricky one."

Luna's eyes widened. "What kind of challenge?"

Dr. Byte appeared on their screens, looking serious. "Kids, meet Hackster. He's a mischievous hacker who loves creating chaos in the digital world. Unlike Phisher, who tries to trick you with emails, Hackster tries to break into systems and cause trouble."

As Dr. Byte spoke, a figure appeared in front of them. Hackster was a small, sneaky-looking character with a hoodie pulled over his head. He had a mischievous grin and a device that looked like a high-tech remote control.

"Well, well, well," Hackster said, his grin widening. "If it isn't the so-called Cyber Heroes. Ready to face a real challenge?"

Max and Luna exchanged determined looks. They knew they had to be prepared for anything Hackster might throw at them.

Hackster's Plan

Hackster held up his remote control and pressed a button. Instantly, the peaceful digital world around them started to change. Data streams turned red and began to flow erratically. Icons flickered and disappeared. The sky darkened, and the ground beneath their feet shook.

"What's happening?" Max shouted, trying to keep his balance.

Hackster laughed. "I'm just getting started! I've planted malware all over the digital world. It will cause systems to crash, data to be stolen, and chaos to reign. And there's nothing you can do to stop me!"

Luna looked around in alarm. "We have to do something, Max!"

Dr. Byte nodded. "Stay calm, kids. We can deal with this. Remember what you've learned."

Max took a deep breath. "Okay, we need to find and remove the malware. But how?"

Cyber Guide fluttered to a nearby console. "We'll need to check each system for signs of malware. Look for anything unusual or out of place."

Max and Luna split up, each taking a different part of the digital world to inspect. They looked for the telltale signs of malware that Dr. Byte had taught them about—strange files, unexpected changes, and odd behaviors.

As they worked, Hackster continued to press buttons on his remote control, trying to create more chaos. But Max and Luna were determined. They used their knowledge to identify the malware and remove it one by one.

Max found a series of strange files in a data stream that was behaving oddly. He quickly flagged them for removal, using the tools Dr. Byte had provided.

Luna discovered that some of the icons were hiding malicious code. She carefully extracted the code and neutralized it, ensuring it couldn't cause any more harm.

Dealing with Hackster

Despite their efforts, Hackster wasn't giving up. He pressed another button, and a new wave of malware spread across the digital world. This time, it targeted the communication systems, causing screens to flicker and messages to scramble.

"We need to stop him for good," Max said, determination in his eyes.

Dr. Byte appeared beside them. "I have an idea. If we can get close enough to Hackster, we can use this special program to disable his remote control. But it won't be easy. He's very quick and slippery."

Max and Luna nodded. "We'll do it," Luna said firmly.

Cyber Pet barked in agreement, ready to assist. Cyber Guide provided them with the special program, a glowing blue icon that Max held carefully.

"Stay together and move quickly," Dr. Byte advised. "I'll guide you as best as I can."

Max and Luna, with Cyber Pet at their side, approached Hackster cautiously. They had to dodge flickering data streams and navigate around areas affected by malware.

Hackster saw them coming and grinned. "You think you can stop me? Good luck!"

He pressed more buttons, causing barriers to appear and block their path. But Max and Luna were determined. They used their knowledge to bypass the barriers and continued their approach.

As they got closer, Hackster started to panic. "No! Stay back!"

Max held up the glowing blue icon. "This ends now, Hackster!"

With a swift move, he activated the special program. A beam of blue light shot out, hitting Hackster's remote control. The device sparked and fizzled, and the barriers disappeared.

"No! What have you done?" Hackster cried out as his remote control fell to the ground, useless.

Dr. Byte appeared beside them, smiling proudly. "You did it, Cyber Heroes! You stopped Hackster and saved the digital world from his chaos."

Max and Luna breathed a sigh of relief. They had faced a tough challenge, but they had overcome it together.

Hackster, now powerless, looked at them with a mix of anger and defeat. "You may have stopped me this time, but I'll be back!"

Max shook his head. "And we'll be ready for you, Hackster. We're Cyber Heroes, and we'll protect the digital world from anyone who tries to harm it."

Luna nodded. "That's right. We've learned a lot, and we're not afraid to use our knowledge to keep the digital world safe."

Hackster glared at them one last time before disappearing into the shadows.

Dr. Byte clapped his hands. "Excellent work, Max and Luna. You've shown great bravery and skill. Remember, the key to dealing with hackers like Hackster is to stay vigilant and use your knowledge wisely."

Max and Luna smiled, feeling a deep sense of pride. They had faced a real hacker and come out victorious.

"Thank you, Dr. Byte," Max said. "We couldn't have done it without your help."

Dr. Byte shook his head. "The credit goes to you, Cyber Heroes. You've proven yourselves time and again. Now, go and enjoy the digital world, knowing that you've made it a safer place."

Max and Luna, along with Cyber Pet and Cyber Guide, continued their journey through the digital world. They knew there would be more challenges ahead, but they felt ready to face them together.

As they walked, they shared a moment of reflection. They had come a long way from their first encounter with phishing scams and malware. They had grown stronger and more knowledgeable with each challenge.

Max looked at Luna and smiled. "We've learned so much. I can't wait to share it with our friends and help them stay safe too."

Luna nodded. "Being a Cyber Hero is about more than just protecting ourselves. It's about helping others and spreading what we've learned."

With renewed determination, Max and Luna continued their journey, ready to face whatever the digital world had in store for them.

Chapter 7: Strengthening Defenses

Learning Advanced Techniques

Max and Luna were excited about their success in stopping Hackster. They had proven themselves as true Cyber Heroes. But they knew there was still much to learn to keep the digital world safe.

Dr. Byte appeared on their screens with a warm smile. "Hello, Max and Luna! You've done an excellent job so far. Now, it's time to learn some advanced cybersecurity techniques to strengthen your defenses."

Max and Luna listened eagerly. They wanted to be as prepared as possible for any future threats.

"First," Dr. Byte began, "let's talk about creating strong passwords. A strong password is like a strong shield that protects your personal information from hackers."

The screen showed a colorful image of a shield with various letters, numbers, and symbols. Dr. Byte continued, "A strong password should be long, include a mix of uppercase and lowercase letters, numbers, and special characters like '!', '@', and '#'. It should also be something unique and not easily guessed."

Max raised his hand. "But how do we remember such complicated passwords?"

Dr. Byte smiled. "Good question, Max. One way is to use a passphrase, which is a combination of words that you can remember but is hard for others to guess. For example, 'BlueCatJumping123!' is a strong passphrase. It's long, has a mix of characters, and is something you can picture in your mind."

Luna nodded thoughtfully. "That makes sense. So, we should avoid simple passwords like 'password123'?"

"Exactly," Dr. Byte replied. "Simple passwords are easy for hackers to guess. Always make your passwords as strong as possible."

Dr. Byte then showed them how to create a strong password using a fun, interactive tool. Max and Luna practiced making their own passwords, combining different elements to create secure and memorable passphrases.

"Great job!" Dr. Byte said after they had practiced. "Now, let's move on to recognizing secure websites."

The screen changed to show two websites side by side. One had a padlock icon and 'https://' in the address bar, while the other did not.

"A secure website uses encryption to protect your information," Dr. Byte explained. "Always look for the padlock icon and 'https://' in the address bar. If you don't see these, the site might not be safe."

Max leaned in to get a closer look. "So, if we see a website without these, we shouldn't enter any personal information?"

"That's right," Dr. Byte confirmed. "Always make sure the website is secure before entering any personal details like your name, address, or passwords."

Dr. Byte also taught them about checking the website's URL carefully. "Sometimes, hackers create fake websites that look very similar to real ones. Double-check the URL to make sure it's correct. If it looks even a little bit different, it might be a phishing site."

Luna raised her hand. "What if we can't tell if a site is safe or not?"

Dr. Byte nodded. "When in doubt, ask an adult or a trusted friend for help. It's always better to be safe than sorry."

Practice Makes Perfect

With their new knowledge, Max and Luna were ready to practice these advanced techniques. Dr. Byte had prepared a series of fun scenarios for them to apply what they had learned.

"Let's start with creating strong passwords," Dr. Byte said. "I'll give you some examples, and you tell me if they're strong or weak."

The screen displayed a series of passwords. Max and Luna had to decide if each one was strong or weak. They quickly identified the weak passwords, like *"123456"* and *"password,"* and praised the strong ones, like *"DragonFly!82"* and *"Starfish#2022."*

"Great job!" Dr. Byte cheered. "Now, let's create some of your own. Remember to use a mix of letters, numbers, and symbols."

Max thought for a moment and then typed, *"Sunshine$789!"* **Luna** followed with *"Tiger@Mountains42."*

Dr. Byte nodded approvingly. "Excellent passwords! They're strong, memorable, and unique. Well, done!"

Next, it was time to practice recognizing secure websites. Dr. Byte set up a virtual environment where Max and Luna had to navigate through different websites and decide if they were secure.

The first website had a padlock icon and 'https://' in the address bar. "Is this site secure?" Dr. Byte asked.

Max and Luna nodded confidently. "Yes, it has the padlock and 'https://'."

"Correct!" Dr. Byte said. "Always look for those signs."

The second website looked similar but had no padlock and only 'http://' in the address bar. "What about this one?"

Luna shook her head. "No, it's not secure. There's no padlock and it's missing the 's' in 'https://'."

"Exactly," Dr. Byte confirmed. "Avoid entering personal information on sites like these."

The final website had a URL that was very close to a well-known site but with a small difference. "Is this site safe?" Dr. Byte asked.

Max squinted at the screen. "It looks almost right, but something seems off. The URL is slightly different."

Dr. Byte smiled. "Good catch, Max. Always double-check the URL to make sure it's the correct one."

Max and Luna navigated through several more scenarios, each time applying their knowledge to determine the safety of the websites. They grew more confident with each practice round, feeling proud of their growing skills.

Dr. Byte then presented a more complex challenge. "Now, let's combine everything you've learned. You'll encounter a series of situations where you need to create strong passwords and recognize secure websites."

Max and Luna nodded, ready for the challenge. They were presented with a series of virtual tasks. First, they had to create a strong password for a new account.

Luna typed, "Galaxy$Skywalker75!" Max followed with "Robot#Universe88." Dr. Byte gave them a thumbs-up for their creative and secure passwords.

Next, they had to navigate through a maze of websites to find the correct, secure site for downloading a game. Along the way, they encountered several fake sites with subtle differences in their URLs. Max and Luna carefully checked each one, identifying the real site by its padlock icon and correct URL.

"You're doing great!" Dr. Byte encouraged them. "Remember to stay vigilant and use all your senses."

In the final task, they had to enter a secure area by deciphering a code. The code was hidden in a series of clues that required them to use their knowledge of strong passwords and secure websites.

Max and Luna worked together, combining their skills to solve the clues and unlock the secure area. They felt a surge of pride as they succeeded in the final task.

Dr. Byte appeared before them, clapping his hands. "Congratulations, Cyber Heroes! You've mastered advanced cybersecurity techniques and proven your skills. You're now even stronger defenders of the digital world."

Max and Luna beamed with pride. They had learned so much and felt ready to take on any challenge that came their way.

"Thank you, Dr. Byte," Max said. "We couldn't have done it without you."

Dr. Byte smiled warmly. "The credit goes to you, Max and Luna. You've shown great determination and intelligence. Keep practicing and stay vigilant. The digital world needs heroes like you."

Max and Luna waved goodbye to Dr. Byte, Cyber Pet, and Cyber Guide as they left the virtual training ground. They felt more confident and knowledgeable than ever before.

Back in their room, Max and Luna looked at each other and smiled. They knew they were ready to face any cyber threat and help others stay safe online.

Luna grinned. "Let's share what we've learned with our friends. The more Cyber Heroes, the better!"

Max nodded. "Absolutely. We'll make sure everyone knows how to create strong passwords and recognize secure websites."

With that, Max and Luna set off on their next adventure, ready to spread their knowledge and protect the digital world from any threats. They were true Cyber Heroes, and their journey was just beginning.

CHAPTER 8: THE FINAL BATTLE

Phisher and Hackster Team Up

Max and Luna were proud of their progress as Cyber Heroes. They had faced phishing scams and malware and learned advanced cybersecurity techniques. But their greatest challenge was yet to come.

One day, as they explored the digital world, Cyber Pet started barking urgently. Max and Luna looked around, trying to figure out what was wrong.

"What's going on, Cyber Pet?" Max asked, patting the robotic dog to calm him down.

Cyber Guide flew down, his eyes filled with concern. "We have a serious problem, kids. Phisher and Hackster have teamed up. They're planning a big attack on the digital world."

Luna gasped. "Phisher and Hackster together? That's really bad!"

Dr. Byte appeared on their screens, looking more serious than ever. "Yes, Luna. They've joined forces to create a powerful threat. They're planning to spread a new type of malware that can steal personal information and cause systems to crash."

Max clenched his fists. "We have to stop them. But how can we fight both of them at the same time?"

Dr. Byte nodded. "It's going to be tough, but I believe in you. With the skills you've learned and the help of your friends, you can defeat them. Let's gather our team and come up with a strategy."

The Cyber Heroes' Strategy

Max and Luna quickly called a meeting with their friends in the digital world. Cyber Pet and Cyber Guide were there, along with some new allies they had made during their adventures.

First, there was Data Defender, a character who specialized in protecting information and stopping data leaks. Then there was Firewall Fox, a clever fox who could create strong barriers to keep malware out.

"Thank you all for coming," Dr. Byte began. "Phisher and Hackster are planning a major attack. We need to come up with a strategy to stop them."

Max stepped forward. "We need to divide our efforts. Phisher and Hackster will likely attack from different directions. We'll need to counter both of them at the same time."

Luna nodded. "Max and I will focus on Phisher. Cyber Pet, you stay with us and help sniff out any phishing attempts."

Cyber Pet barked in agreement, ready for action.

Dr. Byte turned to Data Defender and Firewall Fox. "You two will work with me to handle Hackster. We'll set up barriers and protect the key systems from his malware."

Data Defender and Firewall Fox nodded; their expressions determined.

Cyber Guide fluttered to a perch where everyone could see him. "I'll provide information and updates to both teams. Communication will be key to our success."

With their plan in place, the Cyber Heroes felt ready. They knew it wouldn't be easy, but they were determined to protect the digital world from the combined threat of Phisher and Hackster.

The Showdown

The digital world was unusually quiet as Max, Luna, and their friends prepared for the final battle. They could feel the tension in the air, knowing that Phisher and Hackster were out there, planning their attack.

Cyber Heroes

Suddenly, the sky darkened, and the ground beneath their feet began to tremble. Phisher and Hackster appeared, each holding a device that emitted dark, ominous energy.

"Welcome, Cyber Heroes!" Phisher sneered. "We've been expecting you."

Hackster laughed wickedly. "You may have stopped us before, but together, we're unstoppable!"

Max and Luna stood tall, ready to face the villains. "We won't let you harm the digital world!" Max shouted.

Luna nodded. "We've learned a lot, and we have our friends to help us. You're going down!"

Phisher and Hackster exchanged glances and then activated their devices. A wave of dark energy spread across the digital world, causing data streams to turn red and systems to glitch.

"Let's move!" Max called out. "Stick to the plan!"

Max, Luna, and Cyber Pet focused on Phisher. They knew he would use phishing scams to try and trick them. Phisher pulled out his fishing rod and cast multiple lines, each one carrying a fake email or pop-up ad.

"Don't let him distract you!" Max shouted.

Cyber Pet barked and sniffed out the phishing attempts. Max and Luna quickly identified the fake emails and pop-ups, closing them before they could cause any harm.

Phisher growled in frustration. "You're getting better, but you can't stop all of them!"

Meanwhile, Dr. Byte, Data Defender, and Firewall Fox were dealing with Hackster. Hackster's device emitted waves of malware, trying to break into key systems and steal information.

"Set up the barriers!" Dr. Byte commanded.

Firewall Fox created strong firewalls to block the malware, while Data Defender worked to protect sensitive information from being stolen.

Hackster laughed. "You can't keep this up forever!"

Dr. Byte smiled confidently. "We'll see about that."

The battle raged on, with both sides using all their skills and knowledge. Max and Luna continued to counter Phisher's phishing attempts, while Dr. Byte and his team held off Hackster's malware.

Suddenly, Max noticed something. "Luna, look! Phisher's device is connected to Hackster's. If we can disable one, it might weaken the other!"

Luna's eyes lit up with understanding. "You're right! Let's go for Phisher's device."

They moved closer to Phisher, dodging his phishing lines and pop-ups. Cyber Pet led the way, sniffing out the safest path.

"Now!" Max shouted.

Luna threw a special program they had prepared, aiming for Phisher's device. The program hit its mark, and Phisher's device sparked and fizzled.

"No!" Phisher cried out as his device shut down.

Instantly, the dark energy around Hackster's device weakened. Dr. Byte saw the opportunity. "Firewall Fox, Data Defender, now's our chance!"

Firewall Fox strengthened the firewalls, and Data Defender launched a counterattack against Hackster's malware. The combined effort overloaded Hackster's device, causing it to shut down as well.

Hackster screamed in frustration. "This can't be happening!"

Max and Luna regrouped with their friends, their hearts pounding with adrenaline. They had done it. They had stopped Phisher and Hackster's combined attack.

Dr. Byte appeared before them, beaming with pride. "You did it, Cyber Heroes! You stopped the villains and saved the digital world once again."

Phisher and Hackster, now powerless, glared at the Cyber Heroes. "You may have won this time," Phisher spat. "But we'll be back!"

Hackster nodded. "And next time, we'll be even stronger."

Max stepped forward, his eyes blazing with determination. "And we'll be ready. We've learned so much, and we'll keep learning. The digital world is under our protection."

Luna nodded. "We'll always stand up against cyber threats, no matter how big or small."

Phisher and Hackster disappeared into the shadows, defeated but not giving up. The digital world began to return to normal, the dark energy dissipating and the data streams flowing smoothly again.

Max and Luna looked at each other and smiled. They had faced their biggest challenge yet and emerged victorious.

Dr. Byte gathered them all together. "I'm so proud of you all. You've shown great courage, teamwork, and intelligence. Remember, the key to staying safe is to always stay vigilant and use your knowledge wisely."

Cyber Pet barked happily, and Cyber Guide fluttered down to join the group. Data Defender and Firewall Fox nodded in agreement.

"We couldn't have done it without everyone's help," Luna said, looking at their friends with gratitude.

Max nodded. "That's right. Together, we're stronger."

Dr. Byte raised his hand. "Now, let's celebrate our victory and remember the lessons we've learned. The digital world is safe because of heroes like you."

Max and Luna felt a warm sense of pride and accomplishment. They knew their journey as Cyber Heroes was far from over, but they were ready for whatever came next.

"Thank you, Dr. Byte," Max said. "For everything."

Dr. Byte smiled. "The journey of a Cyber Hero never truly ends. Keep learning, keep protecting, and keep helping others. The digital world will always need heroes like you."

Max and Luna nodded, feeling inspired and ready for their next adventure. They knew there would be more challenges ahead, but they also knew they had the skills, the knowledge, and the friends to face them.

As they left the digital world and returned to their room, Max and Luna felt a deep sense of pride. They were Cyber Heroes, and they were ready to continue their mission of keeping the digital world safe for everyone.

With renewed determination, they set off on their next adventure, ready to spread their knowledge and protect the digital world from any threats. Their journey was just beginning, and they were excited to see where it would take them next.

CHAPTER 9: VICTORY AND CELEBRATION

Defeating the Villains

Max and Luna had faced their biggest challenge yet and emerged victorious. With Phisher and Hackster defeated, the digital world began to return to its normal, vibrant state. The dark energy dissipated, and the data streams flowed smoothly once again.

Cyber Heroes

As the digital world healed, Max and Luna took a moment to catch their breath. They looked at each other and smiled, feeling a sense of pride and accomplishment.

Dr. Byte appeared before them, beaming with pride. "You did it, Cyber Heroes! You stopped Phisher and Hackster and saved the digital world once again."

Max and Luna felt a wave of relief wash over them. They had worked hard, used their knowledge, and relied on their friends to overcome the challenge.

"Thank you, Dr. Byte," Max said. "We couldn't have done it without your guidance."

Dr. Byte shook his head. "The credit goes to you, Max and Luna. You've shown great courage, teamwork, and intelligence. You've proven yourselves as true Cyber Heroes."

Cyber Pet barked happily, wagging his tail in excitement. Cyber Guide fluttered down to join the group; his eyes filled with pride.

Data Defender and Firewall Fox nodded in agreement. "You handled the situation perfectly," Data Defender said. "Your quick thinking and bravery made all the difference."

Firewall Fox added, "And you worked together as a team, which is the most important thing."

Max and Luna felt a warm glow of pride. They knew they had made the right choices and were becoming true defenders of the digital world.

Phisher and Hackster, now powerless, glared at the Cyber Heroes. "You may have won this time," Phisher spat. "But we'll be back!"

Hackster nodded. "And next time, we'll be even stronger."

Max stepped forward, his eyes blazing with determination. "And we'll be ready. We've learned so much, and we'll keep learning. The digital world is under our protection."

Luna nodded. "We'll always stand up against cyber threats, no matter how big or small."

Phisher and Hackster disappeared into the shadows, defeated but not giving up. The digital world began to return to normal, the dark energy dissipating and the data streams flowing smoothly again.

Max and Luna looked at each other and smiled. They had faced their biggest challenge yet and emerged victorious.

Returning Home

With the digital world safe once more, it was time for Max and Luna to return to their normal world. They waved goodbye to their friends, knowing they would always have a place in the digital world as Cyber Heroes.

Dr. Byte gathered them together for a final message. "I'm so proud of you all. You've shown great courage, teamwork, and intelligence. Remember, the key to staying safe is to always stay vigilant and use your knowledge wisely."

Cyber Pet barked happily, and Cyber Guide fluttered down to join the group. Data Defender and Firewall Fox nodded in agreement.

"We couldn't have done it without everyone's help," Luna said, looking at their friends with gratitude.

Max nodded. "That's right. Together, we're stronger."

Dr. Byte raised his hand. "Now, let's celebrate our victory and remember the lessons we've learned. The digital world is safe because of heroes like you."

Max and Luna felt a warm sense of pride and accomplishment. They knew their journey as Cyber Heroes was far from over, but they were ready for whatever came next.

"Thank you, Dr. Byte," Max said. "For everything."

Dr. Byte smiled. "The journey of a Cyber Hero never truly ends. Keep learning, keep protecting, and keep helping others. The digital world will always need heroes like you."

Max and Luna nodded, feeling inspired and ready for their next adventure. They knew there would be more challenges ahead, but they also knew they had the skills, the knowledge, and the friends to face them.

As they left the digital world and returned to their room, Max and Luna felt a deep sense of pride. They were Cyber Heroes, and they were ready to continue their mission of keeping the digital world safe for everyone.

With renewed determination, they set off on their next adventure, ready to spread their knowledge and protect the digital world from any threats. Their journey was just beginning, and they were excited to see where it would take them next.

Spreading the Word

Back in their normal world, Max and Luna couldn't wait to share their adventure and the lessons they had learned with their classmates and teachers. They knew that spreading the knowledge was just as important as using it themselves.

The next day at school, Max and Luna asked their teacher, Mrs. Collins, if they could share their experience with the class. Mrs. Collins, always supportive of her students, agreed enthusiastically.

"Class, Max and Luna have something very important to share with us today," Mrs. Collins announced. "Let's give them our full attention."

Max and Luna stood at the front of the classroom, feeling a little nervous but mostly excited. They knew how important it was to help their friends stay safe online.

"Hi, everyone," Max began. "Luna and I have been on an amazing adventure in the digital world. We've learned a lot about how to stay safe from cyber threats like phishing and malware."

Luna continued, "We faced some really tough challenges, but with the help of our friends and the skills we learned, we were able to stop the bad guys and protect the digital world."

Their classmates listened intently, eager to hear more about the adventure.

"We want to share some of the most important things we learned," Max said. "First, always create strong passwords. Use a mix of letters, numbers, and symbols, and make sure your password is something unique that you can remember."

Luna nodded. "And always look for the padlock icon and 'https://' in the address bar when you're on a website. If you don't see these, the site might not be safe."

Max added, "Be careful with emails and pop-ups that offer free stuff or ask for personal information. These are often phishing scams trying to trick you into giving away your information."

"And if you're ever unsure about something online, ask an adult or a trusted friend for help," Luna said. "It's always better to be safe than sorry."

Their classmates asked lots of questions, and Max and Luna answered them confidently, sharing all the tips and tricks they had learned from Dr. Byte and their adventures.

Mrs. Collins smiled proudly. "Thank you, Max and Luna, for sharing this important information with us. It's so important to stay safe online, and you've done a wonderful job helping us understand how."

After their presentation, Max and Luna's classmates gathered around them, eager to learn more. They showed their friends how to create strong passwords, recognize secure websites, and avoid phishing scams.

Max felt a deep sense of pride as he helped his friends set up strong passwords. "Remember, your password is like a shield. Make it strong and unique!"

Luna showed her friends how to check for the padlock icon and 'https://' on websites. "Always double-check the URL before entering any personal information. If something looks off, don't take the risk."

Their classmates were grateful for the tips and promised to be more careful online. Max and Luna felt like true Cyber Heroes, knowing they had made a difference.

As they walked home from school that day, Max and Luna reflected on their journey. They had faced tough challenges, learned valuable lessons, and shared their knowledge with others.

"I feel so proud of what we've done," Max said, smiling at Luna.

"Me too," Luna agreed. "We've helped make the digital world a safer place for everyone."

Max nodded. "And we'll keep learning and helping others. The journey of a Cyber Hero never really ends."

Luna smiled. "That's right. There's always more to learn and more people to help."

With a sense of pride and purpose, Max and Luna continued their journey as Cyber Heroes, ready to face any challenges that came their way. They knew that by spreading the word and sharing their knowledge, they were making a real difference in the world.

And so, their adventure continued, filled with new challenges, new friends, and new opportunities to protect the digital world and help others stay safe online. Max and Luna were true Cyber Heroes, and their journey was just beginning.

CHAPTER 10: EPILOGUE – BE A CYBER HERO

Reflecting on the Journey

Max and Luna sat together in their room, holding their tablets and thinking about everything they had been through. They had faced many challenges, learned important lessons, and made new friends in the digital world.

"Can you believe all that we've done?" Max asked, looking over at Luna with a smile. "From dealing with phishing scams to battling malware, it's been quite an adventure."

Luna nodded, her eyes shining with excitement. "And we didn't do it alone. We had Dr. Byte, Cyber Pet, Cyber Guide, Data Defender, and Firewall Fox with us every step of the way."

Max grinned. "And now we know so much more about staying safe online. We know how to create strong passwords, recognize secure websites, and avoid phishing scams."

Luna added, "And we've learned the importance of working together and asking for help when we need it."

They both felt a deep sense of pride. They had grown so much and were ready to face any new challenges that might come their way.

"We really are Cyber Heroes," Max said, feeling a warm glow inside.

Max and Luna decided to write down everything they had learned. They wanted to remember all the important lessons and share them with others. They created a list of the key points:

Create Strong Passwords: Use a mix of letters, numbers, and symbols. Make it something unique and hard to guess.

- Recognize Secure Websites: Always look for the padlock icon and 'https://' in the address bar.
- Avoid Phishing Scams: Be cautious with emails and pop-ups that offer free stuff or ask for personal information.
- Ask for Help: If you're unsure about something online, ask an adult or a trusted friend.
- Work Together: Teamwork and communication are crucial in dealing with online threats.
- Keep Learning: The digital world is always changing, so keep learning and stay updated on new threats.

Encouraging Others

Max and Luna knew that their journey wasn't just about their own growth. They wanted to help others become Cyber Heroes too. They decided to share their knowledge with as many kids as possible.

At school, they organized a special Cyber Heroes Day. With the help of their teacher, Mrs. Collins, they set up fun activities and games to teach their classmates about online safety.

Max stood in front of the class, holding a poster that said "Be a Cyber Hero!"

"Hi, everyone! Today, we're going to learn how to stay safe online and become Cyber Heroes. Are you ready?"

Their classmates cheered and clapped, eager to start.

Luna took over, holding up a colorful chart. "First, let's talk about strong passwords. A strong password is like a shield that protects your information. Use a mix of letters, numbers, and symbols, and make sure it's something unique."

They had their classmates create their own strong passwords using the tips they had learned from Dr. Byte. Everyone had fun coming up with creative and secure passwords.

Next, Max showed them how to recognize secure websites. "Always look for the padlock icon and 'https://' in the address bar. If you don't see these, the site might not be safe."

Luna added, "And be careful with emails and pop-ups that offer free stuff or ask for personal information. These are often phishing scams trying to trick you."

They played a game where their classmates had to identify safe and unsafe websites and emails. Everyone was excited to test their new skills and learn from their mistakes.

Max and Luna's classmates asked lots of questions, and Max and Luna answered them confidently, sharing all the tips and tricks they had learned from Dr. Byte and their adventures.

"We also want to remind you," Max said, "that if you're ever unsure about something online, ask an adult or a trusted friend for help. It's always better to be safe than sorry."

Luna smiled at their friends. "And remember, being a Cyber Hero isn't just about protecting yourself. It's about helping others too. Share what you know and make sure everyone stays safe online."

Their classmates were excited to become Cyber Heroes and promised to practice safe online habits. Max and Luna felt proud knowing they had made a difference.

At the end of the day, Mrs. Collins gathered everyone together. "Thank you, Max and Luna, for teaching us so much about online safety. You've done an amazing job, and I'm sure we all feel more confident now."

Max and Luna beamed with pride. They knew their journey as Cyber Heroes was far from over, but they were ready to help others and continue learning.

In the following weeks, Max and Luna noticed a change in their classmates. Everyone was more cautious online, creating strong passwords, checking for secure websites, and being wary of suspicious emails. They even saw their friends helping each other, just as they had encouraged them to do.

Max and Luna felt a sense of accomplishment. They had not only protected themselves but had also helped others become Cyber Heroes. They knew they had made a real difference.

Final Words from Dr. Byte

As Max and Luna were packing up their things to go home, their tablets buzzed with a new message. It was from Dr. Byte.

"Hello, Max and Luna! I just wanted to congratulate you once again on your incredible journey. You've shown great courage, teamwork, and intelligence. You truly are Cyber Heroes."

Max and Luna smiled at the familiar face of their mentor. They felt a warm sense of pride and accomplishment.

"Remember," Dr. Byte continued, "the lessons you've learned aren't just for you. Share them with others and help everyone stay safe online. The digital world is a wonderful place, but it's important to be cautious and smart."

Luna nodded. "We'll keep spreading the word and helping others, Dr. Byte."

Dr. Byte's smile grew wider. "That's the spirit of a true Cyber Hero. Keep learning, keep protecting, and keep helping others. The journey of a Cyber Hero never truly ends."

Max and Luna felt inspired by Dr. Byte's words. They knew they had a responsibility to continue their mission and make the digital world a safer place for everyone.

"Thank you, Dr. Byte," Max said. "We couldn't have done it without you."

Dr. Byte shook his head. "The credit goes to you, Max and Luna. You've proven yourselves as true Cyber Heroes. I'm so proud of you."

With that, Dr. Byte waved goodbye, and the screen went dark. Max and Luna felt a sense of closure but also excitement for the future.

As they walked home, they talked about all the new things they had learned and the people they had helped. They knew there would be more challenges ahead, but they felt ready to face them together.

When they got home, they told their parents all about their adventures. Their parents were amazed at how much they had learned and were proud of their kids for becoming Cyber Heroes.

"You've done a wonderful job," Max's mom said, giving him a hug. "We're so proud of you both."

Luna's dad nodded. "And we can all learn from you. Thank you for sharing what you know."

Max and Luna felt a deep sense of pride and accomplishment. They knew their journey as Cyber Heroes was just beginning, but they were ready for whatever came next.

That night, as they lay in bed, Max and Luna thought about all the adventures they had experienced and the lessons they had learned.

"We've come a long way," Max said softly. "And we've helped a lot of people."

Luna nodded, her eyes closing as she drifted off to sleep. "And we'll keep helping others. The digital world needs Cyber Heroes."

As they fell asleep, they dreamed of new adventures, new friends, and new opportunities to protect the digital world. They knew that as long as they stayed vigilant, kept learning, and helped others, they would always be true Cyber Heroes.

ABOUT THE AUTHOR

Dr. Valarian Couch is an esteemed cybersecurity expert, mastering the art of safeguarding against evolving cyber threats. With over 15 years of experience, Dr. Valarian has a proven track record in enhancing IT infrastructure security and performance. He is known for his innovative solutions, contributing significantly to improvements in cost savings and user retention.

A passionate advocate for digital privacy and online safety, Dr. Valarian's expertise extends beyond professional realms, enriching the global community through insightful writings and unwavering support for open-source initiatives. A respected leader, Dr. Valarian excels in fostering team collaboration and exceeding organizational goals.

Made in United States
Orlando, FL
12 May 2025